removing

d ubt

in an interview

removing d●ubt

in an interview

a better approach to getting the job you want

Eric C. Hoss

Library of Congress Control Number: 2009900209
ISBN: Hardcover   978-1-4415-0184-4
                   Softcover   978-1-4415-0183-7

Photographs by Bryan Siverly
Editing assistance by Elaine Giermak
Cover design by Jennifer Carmack

Produced by Removing Doubt Inc.
Bloomington, Illinois.

The content of this book is solely the opinion of the author and does not reflect the opinions of any other person or organization.

This book was printed in the United States of America.

To order additional copies of this book, contact:
Xlibris Corporation
1-888-795-4274
www.Xlibris.com
Orders@Xlibris.com
52068

Contents

AFTER THE INTERVIEW 107

CONCLUSION 117

RESOURCES

This book is dedicated to everyone
who wants to get better at interviewing.

Preface

Oh the fun of interviewing!

Almost everyone has had to be interviewed for a job or assignment he or she wants. If you're like most people, you hated the experience. People who have recently been interviewed used words like "stressful," "awkward," "frustrating," and "downright scary" when they described their experience. "The worst experience of my life," one person told me, shaking all over, when describing the trauma she endured. She assured me she would rather "go hungry and beg on the street" before putting herself through another interview.

Others say that they hate the feeling of being "judged" or being "put on the spot." Most feel the interview process is not an accurate reflection of whether they can perform the job they are seeking. Some have said that being interviewed made them the most nervous they have ever been in their lives, and their goals in life are to be interviewed as little as possible to minimize the pain.

Of course, nerves are understandable. In addition to risking potential rejection, you are vying for a job or assignment you obviously want—usually one with more money, a possible promotion, and the potential to make your life better. The interview cuts to the heart of personal self-worth—being told you are good at something and being paid money to support yourself or your family. The perceived roadblock in getting that job is getting through the interview. Literally hundreds of interview candidates have told me, "If I could only interview better, my life would improve!"

Sadly, many do not feel they can actually get better at an interview because all the power seems to be with the interviewer. This could not be farther from the truth.

Much contemporary interviewing training advice often misses the mark about interviewing because it encourages interviewees to primarily focus on "maximizing your strengths," "minimizing your weaknesses," or trying not to sweat or stutter during a job interview.

Although this is not bad advice, it can ignore the underlying reasons many people do not get selected for jobs. If a major doubt remains in the mind of the interviewer regarding if the candidate can perform the job, the doubt is often not completely overcome simply through sharing of strengths or other positive aspects.

Example: Let's suppose the interviewer has a doubt about a job candidate because they do not have a certain college degree or designation. Using contemporary interviewing style, the interviewee would ignore bringing up that potential educational weakness and instead emphasize all his great work history and accomplishments during the interview. However, the doubt about a college degree remains in the mind of the interviewer, and he may reject the candidate despite all the great work history being shared. A better approach would be to address that doubt and explain how the interviewee's work history and outside training can more than make up for the absence of a college degree.

This book is about a new approach to job interviewing that targets "removing doubt" in the eyes of the interviewer as a key way to secure the job you want. It introduces a specific and unique technique for each job interview based on the skills and background of the individual, then targets potential doubts and the ways to remove or at least reduce those doubts.

Although no process is perfect (and there are no guarantees you will always be successful in getting a job with this process), the concepts are simple and have had positive results. This book will give you an easy-to-follow "recipe" to improve your interviewing skills.

In addition, visit the Removingdoubt.com Web site for additional tips and interview stories.

Removing Doubt

It goes without saying that maximizing your strengths and applying strong nonverbal skills are good things to work on for an interview. However, the most often missed part of preparing for an interview happens before the interview is even conducted—identifying what *doubts* may exist in the eyes of the potential employer when you are trying for a new job position. The key is to identify what you should be doing *now* to address and correct those doubts. In my experience, the person who gets the job is usually the one who removes the most doubt from the interviewer and reinforces he or she can perform the job.

Removing doubt is a challenge because it requires the candidate to anticipate doubts the interviewer may have and offer solutions to remove those doubts. It also involves potentially discussing weaknesses (doubts) in an interview, which can be challenging if not done correctly. This book will discuss steps to effectively address doubt.

In every competitive job interview, the interviewers have doubts about the candidates' ability to perform the job. Sometimes doubts are due to the candidates' educational background, work experience, or generated in the interview itself. This requires the interviewees to conduct thorough self-assessments before the interview to determine what doubts the interviewers may have, and have a plan to proactively address them. Leaving doubts unresolved can be detrimental to getting the job.

I have been interviewing job candidates for twenty-five years, and there are common themes that have not changed over the past quarter century. There are *tangible* things that can be done to dramatically improve your chances of succeeding in an interview and getting the job you want. This book addresses a new way to tackle the interviewing process that has been found very successful in addressing the "removal of doubt" to increase the chance of getting the job.

Your goal in an interview should be to identify, address, and remove the doubts that the interviewer may have about your ability to succeed in that job. To help identify these doubts, you will see **DOUBT ALERTS** throughout the book to help share what doubts are being inadvertently created by your actions in an interview. This book provides techniques to help improve your chances of getting the job you want by looking through the eyes of the interviewer at removing doubt.

Often, the person who is hired is the one who leaves the *least* doubt with the interviewers that he or she can perform the job. Your task is to help them actually *see* you being successful in the position.

We will explore what to do before the interview, during the interview, and after the interview.

In this book, you will learn the following:

1. Identify doubt
2. Target and remove doubt before the interview starts
3. Give more complete answers using the innovative hourglass answer style
4. Use mock interviews to your advantage
5. Learn how networking will help open doors for a job and help you identify the slang of the company or department you are interested in
6. Create a Kudos File that will become an invaluable library of your achievements and competencies
7. Drive home a personal theme during the interview
8. Prepare a prewritten outline in a Notes Page for the interview that will give you an added advantage and not force you to memorize all your answers
9. Learn from your mistakes in an interview and get better for the next one by using the postevaluation form
10. Minimize nonverbal mistakes that create doubt
11. Ask the right questions in an interview

To stand out from the competition, the interviewee must do more than just share the high points of his employment background and educational achievements—he must identify and remove the doubt that exists in the mind of the interviewer. If this is done correctly, it goes a long way to getting the job!

This book is written for everyone who hates to interview and wants to take charge of getting the job he or she wants!

Acknowledgments

I would like to thank my reviewers for their invaluable assistance. I also thank Ravi Lothumalla, Bill Toft, Karen Davies, and special thanks to my wife, Terri, for all her help and support throughout the writing and reviewing process.

Why We Often Dread Interviews

There are as many reasons why people hate to be interviewed as there are interviews themselves. Luckily, each of these reasons has a potential solution.

Listed below is each concern with potential solutions. Review the list below, check off your reasons for dreading an interview, and note the chapter that addresses those concerns:

- You don't know enough about the new job.
- You are not sure of the experience or educational background that interviewers are looking for in a candidate.
- You are not sure if you have the correct experience for the position.

Covered in "Networking," page 29

- You are afraid you don't have good examples to share and are not sure which ones you should share.
- You are afraid your examples don't answer specifically what the interviewer is looking for.

Covered in "Kudos File," page 37

- You are not sure what the interviewers will ask.
- You are afraid you won't get any better in interviewing.
- You are afraid you won't understand the lingo of the company or will use the wrong terms.
- You are unsure of company's focus/goals.

Covered in "Research through Job Shadowing," page 45

- You are afraid you will forget to share something during the interview.

Covered in "Notes Page," page 50

- You are not sure how you sound in an interview.

Covered in "Mock Interviews," page 61

- You are not sure how to answer the "Tell me about yourself" question (typically at the beginning of the interview).

Covered in "Common Opening Question," page 72

- You are afraid your answers will be boring.
- You are afraid you won't get your message across.
- You are not sure how to answer the interviewer's questions effectively.

Covered in "Answering Questions with the Hourglass Answer Style," page 76

- You are afraid you will be overly nervous during the interview.

Covered in "Body Language and Nonverbal Communication," page 83

- You are afraid you won't know what questions to ask.

Covered in "Questions to Ask during the Interview," page 87

- You are not sure how to answer, "Is there anything else you want to tell us?" question.

Covered in "Common Closing Question," page 92

- You are not sure what to wear to an interview.
- You are not sure what to eat before an interview.

Covered in "Common Errors and Solutions in an Interview," page 96

- You are not sure how to write an effective thank-you note.

Covered in "The All-Important Thank-You Note," page 112

Before the Interview

Before the Interview

A key aspect of successfully preparing for an interview is the time spent prior to the interview itself. This research should happen long before an interview is even scheduled and is ideally part of an ongoing development plan. The key steps in this section include the following:

- How to Identify Doubt

- Job Search Scenarios of Three Potential Careers

- Networking

- Kudos File

- Research through Job Shadowing

- Notes Page

- Mock Interviews

- Game Plan before the Interview

How to Identify Doubt

Your first task in preparing for the interview is to identify doubts that the interviewer may have about you performing the job. This requires a thorough self-evaluation to see how your skills and background fit what you *think* she wants in the role. Knowing the perceptions of the interviewer allows you to target potential doubts and combat/compensate for them in advance.

Listed below are examples of common interview situations and the doubts they can inadvertently create. The potential remedies are for doubts that exist *prior* to the interview and doubts created *during* the interview due to personality, answers given, or body language. There is an extensive list in appendix A, page 119.

1. **Potential doubts based upon your background prior to the interview**

    These can include past job experience, education training, tenure at your current company (or other organizations), years of experience in the workforce, mobility, and previous termination (when known by interviewer).

Interviewee with lack of work experience

Traits. Resume lists limited work experience or no experience in the area interviewing for.

Potential Doubt. Interviewer may perceive a lack of knowledge in the business area, lack of knowledge about the job you are seeking, or unknown work habits.

Risk. Some candidates apologize for their lack of experience or try to exaggerate their experiences to make them more relevant than they really are. This can reinforce the doubt that the candidate does not understand the job he or she is applying for and, thus, is willing to stretch the truth in a stressful situation.

Remedy. Emphasize similar-type experiences without overselling. Cite examples where you were successful in beginning a job or assignment with little experience.

Interviewee with poor grades in college or lack of success in formal education

Traits. Poor grades in classes relevant to the job or low overall grade point average.

Potential Doubt. Perception the candidate is unfocused or not able to finish assigned tasks. Doubts around the quality of work performed and pride in work completed. Potential concerns about intelligence or tendency for laziness.

Risk. Ignoring the grades (and hoping no one notices) is dangerous and leaves the doubt unaddressed.

Remedy. Emphasize learning outside of formal education and a genuine love of learning new things. Give examples of completion of tasks with quality.

Interviewee with job-hopping or short tenure at jobs

Traits. Has short tenures at multiple jobs.

Potential Doubt. Doubts about longevity and dedication to a career. Doubts about holding your attention span and your tendency to get bored with a job after a short time. Also concerns if you can hold a job or if you have been getting fired frequently.

Risk. Ignoring or downplaying multiple jobs increases doubt. Removing jobs from your resume leaves gaps in the employment timeline.

Remedy. Do not hide the fact you have had many jobs. Give examples of your variety of experiences and how they rounded your background. Mention your love of new challenges and emphasize your desire to settle down and make a career at this company.

2. Doubts created during the interview

These are the doubts from answers given by the interviewee, such as incomplete answers or sharing bad examples, body language and eye contact, overall interview presence, and doubts from questions asked by the interviewee.

Interviewee who is overconfident/arrogant

Traits. Overbearing personality with very forceful body language. Shows aggressive leadership traits.

Potential Doubt. Concern by interviewer that you may be difficult to manage, may not be a team player, and may be only interested in your own success.

Risk. Emphasizing your preference for leadership would reinforce the doubt that you won't work well with others and always want to be in charge.

Remedy. Emphasize your ability to work on a team and share in a team's success.

Interviewee who is underconfident

Traits. Timid, introverted personality, quiet voice, lack of presence, limited eye contact, and limited vocal inflection.

Potential Doubt. Concern you won't take a stand when needed, will shy away from leadership opportunities, or be easily swayed to others' opinions.

Risk. By only emphasizing examples where you were contributing to a team's success can reinforce the doubt that you are not a leader or are not ready to tackle difficult assignments.

Remedy. Your answers should emphasize a willingness to accept risk and share examples when you took on a leadership role. This will help combat any doubt that you are not strong enough to work on a challenging task.

Interviewee who is too relaxed

Traits. Poor posture, sitting too casually during the interview or giving glib answers.

Potential Doubt. Gives perception you are not serious about the job. You may come across as either too confident (you appear certain that you will get the job) or lacking confidence (not prepared for the interview).

Risk. Being yourself and at ease can be a valuable asset in an interview, but some formality is expected.

Remedy. Practice good posture, maintain eye contact, and do not look too relaxed during the interview. When answering questions, don't be glib or informal. Also watch the use of unprofessional slang.

Job Search Scenarios of Three Potential Careers

To help identify the recommended steps in preparing for an interview, consider three potential careers: customer service, technical/business analyst, and a sales position. This book follows three fictitious job candidates going through the steps to remove doubts and get the jobs they want in their careers.

Interview for a Customer Service Job—Rachel

Rachel is seeking a customer service position at a large company. It is an entry-level position primarily in telephone support and offers potential growth opportunities within the company. She has limited experience in customer service but believes she would be a strong candidate.

Interview for an Analyst Job—Thi

Thi is interested in an analyst position with a growing company. She has a college degree in business and a strong technical background. With her background, Thi could serve either in business or a more technical role. For this scenario consider Thi both as an experienced employee seeking a new position in her existing company and also as one who is undergoing an interview with a different company.

Interview for a Sales Job—Steve

Steve has always been interested in direct sales of all kinds and is targeting sales at a local corporation. As with the analyst position, consider Steve is undergoing an interview within his existing company and also with a different company.

Networking

Networking helps improve your understanding of the job.

When most people think of networking, it unfairly conjures negative connotations of cheap politics and "buttering up" the interviewer. Nothing could be farther from the truth. Effective networking is an integral part of researching potential job openings and will also make you better known to those who may ultimately be doing the hiring.

Networking is a skill that many people say they struggle with. The key point in networking is that you do not need to have an outgoing personality to be an effective networker. Networking is better defined as the process of informally getting to know people and learning about jobs and departments/companies even before there are job openings in those areas.

Networking can provide information that helps you relate skills and experiences to the position. It can also give you confidence that you have a good understanding of the job. It can increase your chances of landing a position when there is an actual opening since you have demonstrated an ongoing interest for the position.

Sources of networking could include alumni or friends in the field or industry you are interested in. Many schools give access to alumni names that could be an excellent resource to begin networking relationships.

Networking can also help answer another challenging question that is often asked in an interview:

What do you know about our company or department?

Although this question should be anticipated in an interview, few people give good answers. Not knowing about a company can inadvertently create enormous doubt about your interest in the position. Through effective and ongoing networking and research, you will learn the inside information about the company/department that will help you better answer that very important question.

There are several key things that you can do that will make it easier to network and get the job you want:

1. **Start a file on the company or department you want to work in.**

Create a folder to store all information you find on the company/department. Start doing this right away. Key sections for this folder include the following:

o **Key goals of the organization:**

- What are the company's short- and long-term goals?
- How do your skills and interests support those goals?
- What skills should you be learning to be a good future employee?
- Based on the future direction of the company, what new skills are valuable? (For example, is the company looking to acquire another business or exit a certain market?)

   Source: Key goals of an organization are often available on a company Web site, through annual reports, or through online resources (search engines, business-related sites, etc.). Some people actually contact a company's public affairs department and ask for any news releases from the company. Others buy a single share of stock in a public company to get annual reports mailed to them. In the case of small businesses, this kind of internal information can usually only be determined by speaking with someone currently working for the business.

o **Company history:** What is the background of the company? When was it founded? What are some important company milestones? Most interviewers are proud of their company's history, and understanding it can be critical.

Source: This history is often available on the Internet at a company or department's Web site or through discussions with current employees. However, be careful not to ask about trade secret information.

o **Competitive landscape:** Who are the major competitors for this organization? What is the company market share, and is it increasing or decreasing? The more you understand the competitive environment, the more you remove any doubt that you don't understand the company's business.

Source: The bigger the company, the more likely its competitive information will be available on the Internet. Small companies or businesses may require more on-site research with current employees.

o **Major challenges facing the organization:** It is extremely important to know the current challenges that are facing the organization and how they are being addressed. This can include both competitive and legal challenges (discussed below) but often can be as simple as organizational issues such as impending restructuring plans. Technology changes can also have impacts on many businesses.

Source: You can often learn this from the Internet or news clippings, but any firsthand information and its relevance can also be valuable. Make sure you record this information in the *Kudos Folder* (see page 37) and keep it up-to-date.

o **Legal/compliance issues impacting the organization:** How the organization is incorporated (small business/corporation/ mutual company/partnership) is important to understand. This reinforces that you understand the business and will be a strong contributor rather than an uninformed employee. Other questions include whether there are legislative issues potentially impacting the organization or industry.

Source: The Internet or library can be a good source of this information as is firsthand testimony from current company employees.

o **Social obligations:** Be aware of any social or "green" initiatives promoted by the company you are having an interview with. These are becoming popular within some industries.

o **Departmental structure:** You need to understand how the department you are applying for is formally (and informally) structured. This includes the current supervisors and support staff. You should also understand how the department's structure fits in with the overall organization and its goals.

Source: This is easiest to find when applying for a job within the same company. Otherwise, it can sometimes be available through the human resources or recruiting department upon request.

DOUBT ALERT: Don't look too interested in the politics of a department—it can appear you like political games and may be potentially hard to manage.

o **Major officers of the company:** At the minimum, you should know the chief executive officer's or owner's name and other major officers' names and their general backgrounds. It is also important to understand if there are major stockholders in the company and who they are.

Source: The Internet or library can be a good source of this information as is firsthand testimony from current company employees.

2. Set up informational interviews.

Informational interviews are the reverse of regular interviews where the candidate gets to ask the questions to the decision makers. This involves sitting down with key decision makers and hiring managers to better learn about their department. This is more easily accomplished when applying for a job in a company where you are already employed. If you are applying at a new company, this information can often be found at a job fair or through a company human resources department.

Informational interviews can have several advantages:

o **You will learn firsthand what is happening inside the company/department you are interested in.** This can be invaluable information that you can use in an interview—information your interview competitors may not have. If you better understand the landscape of an organization, it removes doubt that you understand the business you are applying for. It also shows you are enthusiastic about being a potential new employee.

Key Point: Make sure you plan well for the informational interview with questions prepared in advance. Do not simply go in with a blank piece of paper and hope to only take notes.

DOUBT ALERT: Failure to be well prepared in an informational interview can create doubt if you are really interested or prepared for the position.

o **You will learn the lingo or language of the area you want to work in informational interviews.** Never underestimate how helpful it will be to know the "language" and acronyms of a company. When the ultimate goal of an interview is to remove doubt and help the interviewer see you in the actual role she is hiring for, one strong way to do that is to speak the company's language. However, be careful of overusing acronyms during the interview even if it is part of the company language.

DOUBT ALERT: Some companies/departments have a strong focus on the customer; others talk more about costs/expenses. If you overly emphasize customer needs in an expense-driven department, you will create the doubt that you don't understand the importance of cost cutting and how the company may not be able to afford to give the customer everything he or she wants. You may gain a better understanding of the company's mentality through an informational interview.

o **You will let the hiring manager know your interest.** This may be more of a long-term plan, but planting seeds of your interest can be integral in being considered later for a position in the department. When the interview is conducted, you are a familiar face who has taken the extra time to learn about the organization. This is not always an option, but it can be very useful when it is available.

o **You will practice.** Practice asking questions and building relationships at non-job-related events (such as a convention for one of your hobbies, a university event, or a chamber of commerce event). Practicing those skills outside of a possible employment situation will make networking easier.

Job Search—How to Use *Networking*

Interview for a Customer Service Job—Networking

Through networking with existing customer service representatives, Rachel should learn about software tools and procedures that are being used by the company. By talking with others in customer service or through the human resources department, Rachel can learn the organizational structure of the company she wants to work for. Rachel should also understand how the customer service employees are measured. (For example, what is their target for time on each call?) Rachel could also network with people in customer service positions at other companies to learn more about the role.

Interview for an Analyst Job—Networking

For business or technical positions, it's important to understand the organizational challenges and the specific role of the analyst. Thi should network with people in similar positions either at her current employer or at another company, to understand the daily duties of the analyst and important competencies and certifications desired. Informational interviews can be critical in this area to have a strong overall understanding of the company and the job. Through networking, Thi should learn the technical procedures being used at the company.

Interview for a Sales Job—Networking

Networking in sales positions is extremely important as a way to get to know sales management. Steve should research a new position by learning about company goals, specifics of the product being sold, and an understanding of the compensation method for sales. Existing salespeople are good sources of information, but some information is also available on the Internet.

Checklist

Identify at least three friends/relatives that are a resource for networking information. Where possible, set up informational interviews with them to learn about their businesses and to practice networking skills.

◆ _____

◆ _____

◆ _____

Review the following information on the Web site of the company you are interested in working for:

◆ Goals

◆ Company history

◆ Major officers of the company

◆ Challenges facing the company (including competition)

◆ Most recent financial information

In the case of a nonpublic company, schedule a meeting with an employee of the business to network and learn details about the business.

◆

_____

Kudos File

The Kudos File helps prevent giving
bad or incomplete answers!

Every day employees accomplish tasks that demonstrate competencies that will be the very foundation for future answers in a job interview. These examples can be from very basic day-to-day work or personal activities to highly important projects with major impacts. Very often, the problem is that over time, people forget all the details that these examples have on work performance. These details make excellent stories to share in an interview.

The Kudos File is a simple and long-term way to combat memory limitations and effectively organize accomplishments for sharing in a future interview. It also can identify competencies to focus on for both development and examples used in answering interview questions.

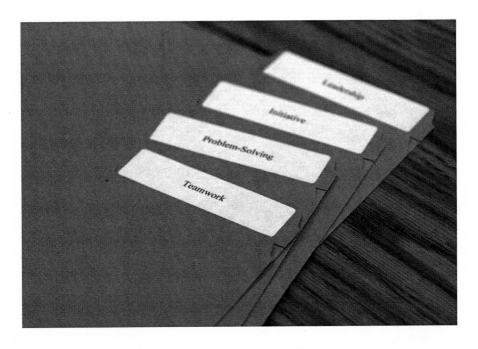

What is a Kudos File?

The *Kudos File* is a folder or series of folders (either electronic or paper) that store your accomplishments, but goes one step farther by organizing the content by competencies (such as leadership, initiative, or team building to name a few). It provides a well-organized history of the work you have accomplished and shares valuable information needed for a behavior-based interview.

Behavior-based questions

A common interview questioning style is the behavior-based interviewing style. This style asks the interviewee about actual experiences he or she have had and how he or she handled certain aspects of the situation. For example, a behavior-based question might be this:

> *Tell me about a time when you had to complete a task with a short deadline? How did you accomplish it?*

With behavior-based questions, the interviewer is looking for a real example (not a theory-based answer of how you might handle the situation if it ever arose). The example being shared is ideally related to the position you are seeking. Unless you are one of the few people who have a photographic memory, the only way to adequately answer questions like these is to have a complete library of examples to share. This library is the Kudos File.

A Kudos File should be an ongoing documentation of your daily work. It should be updated regularly to make sure the most current and best examples are available to share in a potential interview. It provides the user a powerful way to identify which competencies he or she has many examples for and those they need to augment.

There are four easy steps to create a Kudos File:

1. Create individual paper or electronic folders for the most common competencies. Examples include leadership, communication, initiative, problem solving, customer service, team building, etc. Ideally, you should have a folder for each competency and focus on the ones that are most applicable to your career interests. Put these folders in a convenient location.

2. Begin capturing examples that demonstrate each of these competencies as they occur and put them in the folder where they best fit. (In some cases an example may fit in several different folders.) These can be printouts from e-mails or handwritten notes from an event. This should *not* be a time-consuming process—you should simply print off or quickly jot down notes and file them in the Kudos File. The only stipulation is that there needs to be enough detail in your note so you can remember to talk about the example in a future job interview.

   o *Handwritten example: "Had meeting with Joe in accounting, and I recommended a new process to pay bills. Joe thought it would save 10 percent of our current costs . . ."*

   Handwrite this event and store under Problem Solving competency and write the date on the paper. Also note if there is any follow-up on the example needed.

   o *E-mail printed example: "Thanks again for identifying the mistakes in the latest audit and I appreciate your going out of your way to intercept a potentially embarrassing error. Good job."*

In this case, you should print out the e-mail and store it under the Initiative competency and write the date on the paper if it did not print on the e-mail.

3. Once a month, check your Kudos folders to see how many examples you have accumulated for each competency. This will help you identify which competencies you may need to target in your future career development. It is much better to identify deficient areas well before a potential interview rather than at the last minute.

   o   Example: If your Leadership folder has fewer items than other competencies, you should focus on trying to get experiences that will give you leadership opportunities. Sometimes these opportunities are available at work or outside of work (in a charity, sports team, or religious organization). Other options can be from college projects or assignments.

   You should also check the quality of the examples and upgrade where needed.

   DOUBT ALERT: As a general guideline, experiences you are referencing should have occurred within the last eighteen to twenty-four months—anything longer creates the doubt if you have had recent accomplishments. If the accomplishment is very impressive, you may stretch longer than twenty-four months in the example, but this should be a rare instance.

4. When you are ready for an interview, the Kudos File becomes your invaluable library of material to help prepare for the interview questions. Read the examples you have captured, and use them to refresh your memory for the interview. A strong Kudos File provides a great reservoir of your activities to give meaningful, fact-rich examples in the interview that you may otherwise have forgotten.

In addition to helping maintain a great skills inventory for a potential interview, the Kudos File can be an asset in job performance sessions with your supervisor. The difference in the number of details can be huge versus relying solely on your memory to capture your accomplishments. Many supervisors can immediately tell which employees had a well-organized Kudos-like File and those who relied solely on their memory to share their activities and job accomplishments.

Job Search—How to Use *Kudos File*

Interview for a Customer Service Job—Kudos File

Rachel should have examples in the Kudos File that demonstrate her ability to work with customers, excellent teamwork, strong communication skills, and good attention for detail. These examples could come from previous jobs or potentially non-job-related activities.

Interview for a Analyst Job—Kudos File

Thi's Kudos File should have examples that demonstrate her analytical and problem solving abilities. For a recent college graduate, these examples may come from classroom project-related material, but could include work related activities as well. Employers are looking for success in accomplishing tasks as well as understanding the process that was followed to achieve the results.

Interview for a Sales Job—Kudos File

Steve's Kudos File should include his specific role in sales-related activities and their measurable results in exceeding sales targets. These examples should be number-related when possible and demonstrate transferable skills in sales. These examples can be accomplished in college (for a new salesperson) or at a previous job in sales.

Checklist

1. A Kudos File should be an ongoing documentation of your accomplishments and their impact and value. It should be started immediately and not when an interview is imminent.

2. There are four easy steps to using a Kudos File:

   - Create individual folders for common competencies.

     Teamwork
     Initiative
     Communication
     Problem solving
     Leadership
     Accountability
     Judgment
     Analytical thinking
     (other competencies as needed)

   - Capture examples that demonstrate each of these competencies.

   - Periodically review the Kudos folders. Make sure your examples fit into a competency. Otherwise, you may need to create a new folder.

   - Utilize a Kudos folder to identify examples to share in the interview.

Research through Job Shadowing

Learning about a position is critical in removing doubt about getting a job. One great way to do research is through job shadowing. A good job shadowing assignment can differentiate you from others and give you valuable insights for the interview.

A job shadow is a session or period of time where you spend time actually following a person in the current position you are seeking while on the job. Although a job shadow is typically not officially part of the interview, it is naïve to think that your performance in the job shadow may not impact the impressions and doubts with the hiring manager. As a result, make sure all the rules of a job interview (showing up on time, being professional) are followed in the job shadow.

Job shadowing can be difficult when applying for a new company but sometimes is allowed. An applicant can also job shadow at a different company through friends/relatives who perform a similar function to gain perspective on the job he is applying for.

A job shadow offers many advantages:
- Helps you understand firsthand the job you are seeking through personal experience
- Helps you learn the lingo of the job
- Helps you learn any issues or specialties of the job
- Helps you ask questions of current employees to better understand the position
- Helps you confirm this is actually the job you want to apply for. Sometimes it is as valuable to learn of the job you don't want based on the job shadow

A job shadow takes time away from a current employee, so in order to maximize the job shadow experience there are some key steps to follow:

BEFORE THE JOB SHADOW

- Make sure you have researched the job assignment *before* you start the job shadow. You don't want to waste valuable time asking about simple information you could have researched on your own.
- Have a documented plan before the job shadow to determine what you want to learn, how much time you will spend in the job shadow, and how to capture information such as the following:

  o   Key job duties and the skills needed to be successful. For example, if the job involves attending many meetings, make sure you have good note-taking, listening, and organizational skills.
  o   "Unofficial" job assignments that may not be readily noticeable. If there are key liaison duties with another department, make sure you recognize the key interactions and expectations.

DURING THE JOB SHADOW

- Take good notes during the job shadow, but don't be so absorbed in writing that you are not observing the job functions and critical competencies.
- Be respectful of the time of the employee you are shadowing. If an emergency occurs, recognize the employee may not be able to give you his or her attention. In extreme situations, you may need to end the job shadow early.

AFTER THE JOB SHADOW

- Make sure to thank the employee and his or her immediate management both verbally during the job shadow and afterwards in thank-you notes.

Job Search—How to Use *Job Shadowing*

Interview for a Customer Service Job—Job Shadowing

It may be difficult for Rachel to job shadow at an existing customer service operation if she is not employed at that company in another position. An alternative is for her to job shadow at another company through friends/relatives to learn the basics of the job. Through strong networking with existing customer service staff at another company, she can learn the key job skills necessary for a position at the company of interest.

Interview for an Analyst Job—Job Shadowing

If Thi is currently employed at a company, there are more options to job shadow in another department. Spending even half a day with a current analyst would provide great insights into the day-to-day duties. Seeking a job shadow at a different company can be more difficult. In this case, Thi would need to use friends/family to identify an analyst at another company and learn from him or her through a position with similar duties.

Interview for a Sales Job—Job Shadowing

Two key areas for Steve to understand for a sales position includes shadowing an existing salesperson, and to understand the back-office operation. Shadowing an existing salesperson (even in an unrelated field) can provide great insights into learning key sales skills and provide examples to share in an interview. Job fairs can also be a good source of learning about sales positions. Steve should also understand the back-office support system at a company to better understand how orders are processed from the sales department.

Checklist

- Identify three people to job shadow and list their roles. Arrange to job shadow with them.

Person:

_____

Role:

_____

Person:

_____

Role:

_____

Person:

_____

Role:

_____

Using a Notes Page

A Notes Page helps reduce nervousness during the interview and helps ensure that no examples you want to share are inadvertently forgotten.

One of the most debated subjects in interviewing is the concept of taking (or using) notes in a job interview. In this debate, there are two very distinct opinions.

Some job interviewers assert that interviewees should not write or reference any written notes during the interview—in fact, they believe if you choose to take a notebook portfolio into the interview, it should essentially be a prop and not opened or referenced in any way. Remarkably, they believe if an interview candidate references written notes or writes *anything* down, it is detrimental to his or her job interview.

Others (myself included) assert that *limited* references to written notes is OK in an interview. Jotting down a few comments during the interview is acceptable and can dramatically improve the quality of the job interview.

Interviews should not be designed to be memory tests where some interviewers believe using notes is akin to cheating on an exam. At no time in regular employment does management forbid the use of notes (except when taking a test), yet many interviewers believe that an interview is similar to an exam and the only way for the interviewee to honestly succeed is without any written help. Some interviewers boast, "We want you, your memory, and your personality in the interview—that's all."

Being forced to memorize examples and facts for an interview can be a major source of stress. Instead of concentrating on sharing information in a coherent manner, interviewees are forced to recite facts as if they were taking an oral exam.

Without the benefit of written notes, interviewees often give incomplete answers, forget important pertinent facts, and are more nervous as they struggle to remember everything they want to share in the interview. This can create doubt about the quality of their answers in the interview.

Many candidates lament that they forgot to share an important item during the interview and are convinced that was why they did not ultimately get the job they were seeking. With a Notes Page, the chances of forgetting something important are dramatically reduced.

The theory of memorizing interview content and forbidding the use of any notes fails to understand the primary point of a job interview: to hire the right candidate with the best background and skills for the job, not necessarily the one who happens to have the best memory or smoothest communication style under stress.

A one-page Notes Page can assist the interviewee in several ways:

- It ensures that no examples are missed during the interview due to memory lapses or stress.

- It boosts the interviewees' confidence since they don't have to memorize everything they want to share.

- It allows for more complete answers with reminders of the examples to share.

- It should *not* replace solid preparation before the interview but is a complement to help the memory.

Listed on the next page is an example of a Notes Page and the five sections for the interview. The candidate should prepare the Notes Page in advance and have it on the inside first page of his or her portfolio or notebook during an interview.

INTERVIEW NOTES PAGE TEMPLATE

A—List the names of the interviewers here in the order they are sitting across from you. *(Write **during** the interview.)*

B—List the questions you are ASKING the interviewers (have three to four questions ready.) *(Write **before** interview and leave space for their response.)*	D—List competencies and examples here. Use a few words to trigger your memory. *(Write **before** interview.)*
C—Write a question that comes from the *interview* itself. *(Write **during** interview.)*	E—List any other information you would like to share. *(Write **before** interview.)*

Notes Page Section A (Complete DURING the interview)
On this space at the top of the page, write down the interviewers' names in their seated locations relative to you when the interview begins. By writing this down, you can list their names and roles and will reduce your chance of calling someone the wrong name during the interview. In addition, writing the names down of the interviewers can help you understand the context of their questions from the hiring manager versus the human resources manager.

Even if you are sure you know the interviewers' names, writing them down is one less thing you need to remember during the stress of the interview. In the stress of an interview, you may be surprised how your memory will play tricks on you, and you may accidentally call an interviewer by the wrong name.

This section can also be used to write down the job title if it's shared—sometimes it is different from what was originally posted.

Notes Page Section B (Complete BEFORE the interview)
This is where you put the questions you will ask during the interview. As will be discussed later on page 87, these questions should be ones that are not easily answered (such as information that you could have easily learned from a company or departmental Web site). Ideally, list three to four good questions here.

DOUBT ALERT: Asking questions that are too simple or questions that are easily researched could create doubt that you have adequately researched the job.

Notes Page Section C (Complete DURING the interview)
This section is where you write a question you will ask from the content of the interview itself. Asking such a question demonstrates good listening skills and will impress the interviewers that you are actively involved in the interview.

This question typically starts with the phrase to the interviewers, "*You mentioned earlier that . . .*" and is not something you could have prepared for in advance.

Example: The hiring manager mentions to the candidate at the beginning of the interview that the department is researching adding new regions to its area of responsibility. A good question would be this: "*You mentioned earlier that the department is* *considering adding new regions . . . how do you see this role changing as a result?"*

Most candidates prepare canned questions for the interview, but very few actually ask something from the content of the interview itself. This can be a differentiator and is impressive to the interviewer(s).

Notes Page Section D (Complete BEFORE the interview)

This is usually the most important section—it is where you highlight the competencies and examples you want to bring into focus. The steps for this section include listing competencies with a couple words to remind you of the example you want to give.

Example:

- Team-building (competency)
  o   Texas example
  o   Weber report

- Initiative (competency)
  o   New product marketing idea
  o   Identify tax cost savings

The examples should come from your Kudos File (discussed on page 37). The key words listed serve as memory triggers during the interview to explain your example in detail.

Notes Page Section E (Complete BEFORE the interview)

This section is used to include any other relevant information that doesn't neatly fit in a competency list. Miscellaneous examples written here might include work history you want to highlight, any unique educational experiences, or special skills you feel are most relevant to the job. Ideally, you want as many strong examples as possible to appear under an actual competency, but there are times when examples do not fit neatly into a category.

Writing this information here will ensure that you don't forget to share it during an interview. This section could be useful at the end of the interview when the interviewers ask, "Is there anything you want to share with us?" You can check this section to see if something important did not get covered.

INTERVIEW NOTES PAGE SAMPLE

Pete Jones   Al Ford
                    Mary Doe

Customer service rep interview, May 5, 2008

Q: I noticed on your Web site that growth has averaged 25% per year. What do you attribute that growth to and how do things look in the next three years?	Leadership—Texas project
	Initiative—suggested new billing program
	Teamwork—produced new dept. report
Q: I understand the department is going through a major software upgrade. How is it going, and what are the measures of success for the software?	Problem solving—fixed quality issue with new product line
	Customer service—provided extra help for customer.
Q: Earlier you mentioned the department was getting new software. How do you see that increasing productivity?	Received masters in business administration in 1990

How to Use the *Notes Pages*

Make sure you write the Notes Page neatly (some people actually type the content in advance) so that it doesn't appear to the interviewers you have written scribbles (see Notes Page example on previous page).

1. Before the interview begins, review your Notes Page while you wait to enter the interview room. Ideally, you want to refer to the Notes Page as little as possible during the interview.
2. When the interview begins, ask the interviewers if it's OK to take brief notes during the interview. This will help you determine if they are OK with your Notes Page and reduce your nervousness about using notes.
3. If the interviewers are OK with using notes, *quickly* write down the names of the interviewers on Notes Page section A in the order they are sitting in front of you. Maintain as much eye contact as possible while you are jotting down their names.
4. Sometimes interviewers will hand you a business card, which you can use to spell the names correctly (and use later to write the all-important thank-you notes).
5. During the interview, listen carefully for a question that you will ask from the content of the interview itself and quickly write it down in Notes Page section C. Write sparingly so you don't appear to be taking dictation and lose eye contact. This question will serve as a reminder when the time comes to ask questions of the interviewers.
6. During the main part of the interview, use Notes Page sections D and E for examples to demonstrate competencies or other facts that came from your Kudos File. Use this only as a reminder—do not refer to it unless you need a refresher.
7. Normally I recommend keeping the portfolio closed so you aren't tempted to use the Notes Page as a crutch, but do whatever is comfortable for you. Sometimes the layout of the room can dictate what works best with using the Notes Page.
8. Use Notes Page section B and C to ask your questions at the end of the interview. Make sure you have listened carefully to the content of the interview so you don't ask a question that was already covered.

DOUBT ALERT: If you ask questions that were already covered by the interviewer earlier in the interview, it will raise doubt you are a poor listener. If you ask questions that are easy to find the answer (through a Web site for the department of company) you create the doubt you didn't carefully research (or worse yet, don't understand) the job.

Benefits of the *Notes Page*

- A Notes Page can be a great confidence booster and reduce the chances of "blanking out" during a question due to your stress, nerves, or bad memory. It allows you to concentrate on the interview itself without trying to memorize everything in advance.
- It forces you to organize your thoughts in advance of the interview by writing what you want to share and helps you evaluate the quality of the answers. If there are gaps in your examples, you will know it before the interview itself. Ideally, it works best with a well-documented Kudos File (page 37).
- A well-written Notes Page can dramatically improve the quality of the answers you share, since you have written reminders to ensure that you cover the important examples. Interviewees with a Notes Page generally give better and richer answers that help the interviewers evaluate their experiences.
- The Notes Page becomes a great review tool after the interview. You can use the page to review what questions went well, what answers you need to update, and what was missing. The Notes Page for each interview should be dated and stored in the Kudos File for future reference at upcoming interviews.

Cons of the *Notes Page*

One of the major cons of the Notes Page is that some interviewers don't like the candidates to have any kind of notes during the interview. It is difficult to know in advance if the interviewer has this bias. However, I think in many instances the risk is worth taking since the alternative is to give incomplete answers to a question.

In all the interviews I have conducted, I have never known a person to *not* be offered a job because he or she were referring to notes, but I do know many people who didn't get offered the job because they gave poor or incomplete answers. The Notes Page is a great antidote for avoiding bad or incomplete answers. It also helps to prevent forgetting an important aspect of your background during the interview.

In summary:
- The Notes Page can be a valuable tool to prepare for an interview.
- It can be a great stress reliever during the interview by reducing the need to memorize all the examples in advance. That alone will add confidence and help remove doubt you are a well-prepared job candidate.
- It should be kept to a maximum of one page (you should not turn pages during the interview).
- Clearly write (or type) your Notes Page so it doesn't appear messy during the interview.
- Write sparingly on the Notes Page during the interview itself so you don't risk having poor eye contact or forget the point of the interviewers' question.
- By writing down the names of the interviewers you will reduce the chances of calling someone by the wrong name. This will be valuable in making sure that the thank-you notes go to the right people. (See page 112 on thank-you notes.)
- The Notes Page should be used during mock interviews (page 61) to assess any changes that you should make.
- In the rare instance when you ask to use notes, and the interviewer is adamant against the use of notes, you should not refer to them during the interview. However, in this situation, organizing your thoughts in advance with a Notes Page is still valuable for preparation even if you won't use it during the interview.
- A Notes Page is a great record of the interview and is a valuable learning tool to review what worked and what didn't work. File the Notes Page in your Kudos File for future reference.

On the next page is a blank Notes Page to use in an interview.

Mock Interviews

Mock interviews are a great way
to practice your skills before an interview.

One of the best ways to practice for an actual job interview is through mock (practice) interviews. This gives the candidates a chance to practice their skills and receive constructive recommendations for improvement. It is always better to find out potential problems during a mock interview rather than in the real interview itself.

Although many people engage in a mock interview, they often do not maximize the experience. There are several ways to get the most out of a mock interview:

- Mock interview with someone you do not know very well. Although there is comfort in having an interview with someone familiar, that comfort could be detrimental to getting constructive and direct feedback.
  - o Someone familiar to you—including spouses, family members, a current boss, or even coworker friends—may not identify quirks that could hurt you in the interview. They also may not be as honest for fear of hurting your feelings or lowering your self-confidence for the interview. Mock interviewing with someone who will be unbiased will pay dividends in being better prepared for the actual interview.

    Example: If you usually speak quickly, people familiar to you have likely become accustomed to your fast rate of speech and will not recognize it is a potential problem. However, if you have the interview with someone who doesn't know you well, that person could identify the concern as something that should possibly be fixed.

- The mock interview should be as realistic as possible including dressing formally as if it were a real interview. This may include practicing for the estimated length of the real interview.

   o Although these suggestions may seem extreme, the best way to simulate a real interview is with formal clothing and all its constraints. Mock interviewing in shorts and a T-shirt may seem easier, but it will not prepare you once the real interview occurs when you wear more formal clothes. I have known candidates who try to have their mock interview in the actual room where the interview will be held, so it is as close to a "dress rehearsal" as possible.

- Based on the job you are being interviewed for, set goals for each question of the mock interview by letting the mock interviewer know what to look for and see if it was accomplished with your answer. This involves putting yourself in the eyes of the interviewer and deciding what you want her to feel about you after the interview. These goals are determined after the question is asked by the interviewer—it is important the mock interviewer selects the questions, not you.

   Example: If you are being asked a question regarding your ability to work under pressure, plan what message you may want conveyed to the interview team. In this case, you want them to feel you are able to handle pressure, think clearly, and make good decisions. Before the mock interview, list these goals you want to accomplish for this question and ask the mock interviewer if you succeeded in conveying that message to him.

- Even when the mock interviewer is asking questions you did not supply, it is important to review your answers and make sure your messages were clear to him or her.

- Practice your answers, but don't make them appear over-rehearsed. Make sure the key points get across with a goal of removing any potential doubt.

- Align your answers with an overall strategy to be successful. I am constantly amazed at how many interview candidates fail to set a goal message for an answer and are then surprised when the meaning of their answer is apparently misunderstood. This goal message should be what you want the interviewer to learn from the example you are sharing.

- Always practice the "Tell me about yourself" (page 72) and "conclusion" (page 92) questions. These are often ignored, and many interviewees struggle with them.

- Videotape your mock interview. This time-honored activity is good suggestion to observe your nonverbal communication during an interview. This can include watching the tape without sound (to focus on your nonverbal communication) and then with the sound added in. It can also be helpful to review answers and see if they make sense and would keep the interviewers' attention.

In summary:

- Mock interviews are a great way to practice your skills prior to an actual interview.

- Make mock interviews as realistic as possible, including dressing for the interview and practicing for the length of an actual interview. Use a Notes Page just as you would in the real interview.

- Mock interview with someone who is not very familiar with you. Interviewing with someone you personally know may not be particularly helpful in getting unbiased feedback. However, it's OK to first have warm-up interviews with family or friends as long as the actual mock interviews are with people who do not know you well.

- Set goals for the mock interview in advance and ask the mock interviewer to evaluate you based on those goals. For example, if you want to have your answers to be more complete, ask the mock interviewer to see if you accomplished that goal.

- Practice the opening question (Tell me about yourself) and closing question in the mock interview.

- Practice and learn from the mock interviews. The only way you will get better is to accept and learn from constructive feedback.

Checklist

- Identify three people to have a mock interview with. Note feedback from each person.

Person:

_____

Role:

_____

Feedback (use separate page)

Person:

_____

Role:

_____

Feedback (use separate page)

Person:

_____

Role:

_____

Feedback (use separate page)

Game Plan before the Interview

A successful job interview is well planned prior to the actual event. It is never too early to start preparing for an interview and target and remove any doubt. Listed below are some recommended steps:

- Have an extensive and dynamic networking group to research areas and jobs you want well in advance of the job opening. Keep in regular contact.

- Create a Kudos File to capture the examples and stories to tell from your experience. Make sure to check it regularly to have the most up-to-date position-related examples.

- Create a theme that leverages examples from the Kudos file with a focus on removing doubt. This will vary based on the job being sought and your background.

- Research the area of interest to ensure good understanding of the job duties. Job shadowing can be an excellent way to learn firsthand about the position you are seeking. In the case of interviewing with a new company, consider job shadowing with a friend/relative from another company who has similar job duties to the position you are seeking. Also make sure to be familiar with any Web sites for the company/department and recent articles or issues about it.

- Make sure you know the key competencies of the job you are seeking. Have strong examples from your Kudos File that demonstrate why you should be hired for the position.

- Create a Notes Page that captures the information you want to share in an interview. Have it prepared in advance.

- Once you have the Notes Page written, participate in mock interviews to practice your skills. Make sure the mock interview is as realistic as possible, including using the Notes Page for your answers.

- If the mock interviewer is asking questions you did not supply, review your answers with her to ensure you are communicating your point effectively.

- Practice writing the thank-you notes as well. If you have a good example of a note, keep it as a template for future thank-you notes.

Following these steps should have you well prepared for the upcoming interview. The next section of this book takes you to the actual interview itself.

During the Interview

During the Interview

For most job candidates, the actual interview gets the majority of the attention and planning. This next section lists the top steps to prepare for the actual interview itself:

- Common Opening Question: "Tell me about yourself"

- Answering Questions with the Hourglass Answer Style

- How to Leverage Body Language and Nonverbal Signals

- Questions You Ask during an Interview

- Common Closing Question: "What else do you want to share?"

- Common Errors in an Interview and How to Avoid Them

Common Opening Question: "Tell Me about Yourself"

*This is an important first question—make sure you can
effectively talk about yourself to start the interview well!*

One of the most difficult questions in an interview for many
should be one of the easiest. Typically it's one of the first questions
and is "Tell me about yourself."

This should be easy because it's a subject each person is,
without a doubt, the expert on—after all, no one knows us better
than we know ourselves! However, there are many reasons why
this question causes concerns among many candidates and is often
handled badly in the interview.

Some reasons why this question can be so difficult include the
following:

1. *"I don't like talking about myself."*
2. *"Where do I start?"*
3. *"I don't know what they are looking for."*
4. *"How much detail do they want?"*
5. *"Should I discuss my personal life or just work history?"*
6. *"How long should the answer be?"*
7. *"Do they really care—isn't this just a meaningless question?"*

From the interviewers' point of view, the usual objective of this
question is to serve as an icebreaker (before the tougher interview
questions begin), but it can serve as a powerful first impression while
the interviewers are the most attentive. As a result, this question
should *not* be treated lightly and does demand advance preparation.
Although this question is very common in most job interviews, it is
amazing how few people actually prepare their answer in advance
(and it often shows).

In some interviews, the interviewer is looking at the content of
the first question and also the way the answer is delivered. This
can be especially important in sales or customer service-related
positions that require strong communication skills.

There are many ways to handle this question, but listed below
are some things worth doing:

- Highlight main points tied to your professional career
- Limit personal information
- Keep it short (three to four minutes maximum)
- Create a "theme" about yourself (more on this later)

The biggest "don't" is the very common tendency to answer the question like an oral resume (listing dates and jobs *chronologically* from the least recent to most recent job held).

Example: Consider the case of Jane Jones who is seeking a supervisory position at a customer call center.

> *Chronological answer: "I started at* _____ *Company in 1990 and worked five years in technical support before moving in 1995 to the customer service division for three more years. After that, I worked six months at another call center, followed by . . ."*

This common approach has several negatives:

- It is expressing information that was likely already provided on a resume. It can be a waste of valuable interview time.
- It can be downright boring (how many people liked memorizing dates in school?).
- It does not "sell" you or effectively remove doubt.
- It can be an awkward start to an interview and risks not capturing the interest of the interviewers.

A better approach is to wrap your job history into a "theme" that captures the essence of you and immediately starts the important "selling" process of the interview. Using the previous example of Jane Jones, a theme-based answer would focus on Jane's background as support for her new position.

Example: Jane has worked in customer service her entire career and now is seeking a supervisory position in a customer call center. A different way to start the "Tell me about yourself question" is using a theme-based answer.

> *Sample theme-based answer: "I have been serving the customers of our company my entire career at* _____

Company and in my opinion there is no more important job than to ensure their needs are met. I have used my strong customer service skills in many areas at our company and want to apply my skills in a leadership position where I could coach other employees on my experiences and best practices. I first learned these skills in a technical support position in 1990..."

The theme-based introduction has many advantages compared to the chronologically based answer:

- It sells the theme about Jane's interest and expertise in customer service and why it would be a logical next step for her to be a supervisor in that area.
- It does not bore the interviewers with a lot of facts but instead tells a story that explains the result (which is usually far more interesting for the listener).
- Jane could cover the actual dates of her job history after setting up the main theme of customer service without making it her main point. (Interviewers hire people, not resumes.)
- A theme-based answer is a better icebreaker since it is conversational in tone rather than the formal tone of the date-driven chronological answers.

There are five easy principles to the "Tell me about yourself" answer in the theme-based approach:

- o Based on your job background and interests, create a theme to introduce yourself.
- o Follow-up with pertinent details as needed.
- o Limit rattling off dates; instead, highlight why the work experience is relevant to this potential job assignment. If the interviewer wants more detail on a specific job you have held, he or she will ask.
- o Keep your answer short (three to four minutes maximum)—it is an icebreaker and not designed to highlight *everything* on your resume.
- o Conclude with an explanation of why this job is a logical next step in your career development and that you are excited about the position and ready to take on the assignment.

Checklist

• Practice writing the "Tell me about yourself" question.

Theme: _____

_____

_____

_____

Pertinent Details: _____

_____

_____

_____

Conclusion: _____

_____

_____

_____

Answering Questions with the Hourglass Answer Style

Answering questions with the hourglass answer style
gives better, more interesting answers.

One area that candidates seem to worry most about in an interview is answering the questions effectively. Unfortunately, the traditional way of answering questions is often the least effective way to communicate since it is often telling a story when the most important information is buried at the end (when the result is eventually realized and shared). It is important to understand a common questioning style in an interview—the behavior-based question.

Behavior-based question

As discussed in the Notes Page on page 50, many interview questions will be behavior based and will seek to understand how the interviewee handled a situation in the past as an indicator of how he or she would handle a similar situation in the future. These questions often start with *"Tell me about a time when "* . . .*"* Unlike a theory-based question that asks more of an opinion about how to handle an event, this question wants an actual *real* event when the interviewee handled a certain situation.

An example of a behavior-based question is this:

Tell me about a time when you worked to complete
something under a tight deadline.

In this case, the interviewers want the interviewee to recite a factual example from his or her recent history (usually within eighteen to twenty-four months) and not a pretend story on how he or she would handle this situation should it occur in the future.

Unfortunately, the temptation to answer this type of question is to answer it chronologically starting with the beginning of the story when often the least important background information is occurring.

Traditional answer to the question "Tell me about a time when you worked to complete something with a tight deadline":

About three months ago, I was assigned a project to write new specifications for our turbines. At first, I gathered the team, researched the specifications, and for two weeks formulated a plan. After another two weeks of research, I had an idea to use new software to write the specifications. After purchasing the new software, and with another week of training, I discovered this approach cut months off the process, and we were able to get the new specifications completed in record time with the same quality.

As this example illustrates, the problem with this common chronological approach to an answer is that the most important information is stuck at the end of the story when the interviewers' attention span is typically the weakest. In addition, it can be more confusing to tie all the details in the story when the final result is at the end.

Luckily, there is a much better way to answer questions we can borrow from journalism—the "inverted pyramid" style and how it leads to the more effective "hourglass" answer style where the important result is first.

We will discuss how you can use this powerful tool in interviews and dramatically improve the quality of your answers by starting your answer with the most important information.

Hourglass Answer Approach

This approach is common in journalist writing where the most important information is at the beginning of the story in a newspaper or magazine. It is used to catch the readers' attention at the beginning and encourage them to continue reading the story. This same successful journalism principle can work very well in an interview with a slight adaptation of adding a strong conclusion at the end of the story (this is usually missing in a newspaper article), creating the interviewing "hourglass" answer style.

The shape of the hourglass gives us the important parts of this answer technique. The wider the hourglass section, the more important part of the answer you are giving.

- The wide top of the hourglass is the first part of the interview answer and should include the important result from the story. This needs to grab the interviewer's attention and refers to the result. It demonstrates the competency the interviewer is asking about.

  - The narrow center of the hourglass contains the less important background details of the example you are sharing. They are relevant to the story but typically not very attention-getting. The details provide support for the result that was accomplished.

- The wide bottom of the hourglass is the conclusion and needs to summarize *your* result and role in accomplishing the goal. This reinforces your message.

An easy way to get used to giving an answer in the hourglass answer style is to first list the key points of every answer.

- Example: In the previous question *"Tell me about a time when you worked to complete something with a tight deadline,"* list the key points you feel are the most important in the example of your role in writing new specifications for the turbines:

  o Recommended new approach (software)
  o Cut months off the development time
  o Had same quality as the older way
  o Meet or beat deadline

This list becomes the introductory paragraph that catches attention of the interviewers.

Hourglass answer introduction approach to the question "Tell me about a time when you worked to complete something with a tight deadline":

I recently recommended using new software that successfully cut months off the time to write new specifications for our turbine with the same quality. This began three months ago . . .

Compare using the hourglass answer approach to the traditional way to answer this question.

Traditional answer (boring) introduction approach:

About three months ago, I was assigned a project to write new specifications for our turbine. First, I gathered the team, researched the specifications . . .

Through this hourglass answer style, the important attention-getting information is brought up first while covering the less important details later in the answer.

The conclusion of the answer (after the details in the middle) is a restatement of the introduction to deliver home the final result. In this example, that could be this:

Hourglass answer conclusion approach:

In summary, my recommendation of the new software was a major success for our company and helped us better compete by successfully cutting months off the time to write new specifications for our turbine with the same quality.

Although the hourglass answer style is a powerful way to capture the attention of the interviewers, it often requires a new thought process for giving answers. The human mind traditionally tells a story chronologically where the result is shared at the end of the story. It takes practice to successfully give answers with this style. However, when mastered, the hourglass answer style can be a strong competitive advantage for the interviewee.

In summary:

- The use of the hourglass answer style gets the most pertinent information first in the answer and not the less important supporting details. It is demonstrating the competency being asked about.

- The background details are given in the middle of the answer. If the interviewer wants more details, they will ask for them.

- The conclusion is a strong restatement of the result and its impact to the situation.

- The hourglass answer style can be an effective way to catch the interviewer's attention and can have a powerful conclusion that reinforces the introduction.

- It takes practice. Our tendency is to recite stories chronologically, which naturally leaves the important result at the end of the story when the interviewers' attention is usually the weakest.

Checklist

- Practice writing an answer using the hourglass style.

Important result from the story (needs to grab attention):

_____

_____

_____

_____

Details to support the result:

_____

_____

_____

_____

Highlight your role in the result and reinforce result:

_____

_____

_____

_____

Body Language and Nonverbal Communication

While the actual choice of words and the content of answers are extremely important in an interview, the nonverbal and body language aspects can be equally important.

Generally, a majority of the communication that occurs between people is nonverbal, such as tone of voice, body language, and overall presence. Many interview candidates feel this is unfair because it seems to put more emphasis on style over substance. In reality, the use of good nonverbal skills can enhance an interview and can go a long way to removing doubt.

There are three major categories of body language and nonverbal communication:

- *Voice.* The tone and intonation of the voice can convey professionalism and assurance or can inadvertently create doubt.

    o   A loud voice can appear dominating or confrontational.
    o   A quiet voice can appear timid and lacking confidence.
    o   A monotone voice by the interviewee can literally lull the interviewers to sleep and risk missing delivering the key message.

A good voice has a storytelling style that maintains the interest of the interviewers, while not distracting from the all-important task of sharing information. Practice in front of a video camcorder or with a tape recorder to see how your voice sounds and work to find the right tone. A good mock interview can also help identify any voice-related issues. (See page 61 on "Mock Interviews.")

- *Body Language.* This broad category covers nonverbal issues during the interview.

    o   A trembling hand can create doubt about your ability to handle pressure. Keeping your hands in your lap can be a way to minimize any distractions from nerves.

o   Sitting in an awkward posture can also be distracting. Appearing too comfortable or relaxed in your posture creates doubt about your seriousness about the interview. Being too rigid (military-like seating) can create doubt about your flexibility in the workplace. A good posture is one that does not attract any attention.

o   Fidgeting with items during the interview can be very distracting. Examples include fidgeting with your pen, watch, or any item on the table.

    ▪   I once had an interviewee who was unknowingly doing acrobatic feats with his pen during the interview. Although I was impressed with his manual dexterity, it was very distracting and tempted me to grab the pen out of his hand.

Using a camcorder can help you to observe what body language you may inadvertently be displaying during an interview. Ideally, you do not want any distractions.

• *Overall presence.* This includes any miscellaneous impressions such as handshakes, eye contact, and your general presence during the interview.

o   Have a good handshake that is not too strong and not too limp. An additional factor is to maintain eye contact and introduce yourself during the handshake.

    ▪   Example: During one interview the candidate shook hands with one person, but was making eye contact with another person in the room at the same time. It was distracting and bordered on being rude. Obviously, this was not a good start to the interview.

o   Eye contact can be very important in an interview and is sometimes handled poorly. Some examples are too little eye contact (eyes drifting away from the questioner) and too much eye contact (fixed on the questioner with a stern stare). Ideally, a mix of focused eye contact with an occasional breaking of eye contact works best.

- Suggestion: If you are in a panel interview with multiple interviewers, have initial eye contact with the person who asked you the question. However, after ten seconds shift your eye contact to the other members of the panel as you are answering the question. As you are ending your answer, return your eye contact to the original questioner. This technique will show the original questioner you respect who asked the question, but you do not exclude the other members in the panel while giving the answer.

In the interest of brevity, only a few of the most common nonverbal situations are listed in this section. Additional examples are outlined in appendix A (page 119). Each interview candidate has his own nonverbal issues to work with, and only through practice can he minimize their negative impact in the interview. The key goal is to ensure that no new doubt is created during the interview.

Job Search—How to Use *Body Language*

Interview for a Customer Service Job—Body Language

Many customer service jobs rely on an effective telephone voice to communicate with customers and will not focus as much attention on nonverbal body language. Rachel should practice a speaking voice that is confident and articulate. Some companies will actually interview the candidate on a telephone in another room to evaluate her speaking style and intonation without the benefit of facial expressions.

Interview for an Analyst Job—Body Language

Thi needs to work both on her verbal skills as well as her nonverbals in the interview. Interviewers will be evaluating how Thi will represent herself in meetings and with team members. Thi should have mock interviews and job shadow where possible to receive feedback on her body language.

Interview for a Sales Job—Body Language

In a sales interview, body language can be extremely important. Steve needs to demonstrate how he would represent the company with a customer through good interpersonal skills. He should have good eye contact, a conversational tone that is confident but not arrogant, and an overall pleasant demeanor. Steve also needs to demonstrate good listening skills when the interviewer is talking.

Questions to Ask during the Interview

Although traditional first impressions of an interview has the interviewee being asked questions, there is one part of the interview where the interviewer turns the tables and the job candidate asks the questions.

Typically at the end of an interview, the interviewers will ask if the candidate has any questions for them. It is extremely important not to ask poor questions or it will inadvertently create doubt with the interviewers.

Preparing good questions to ask the interviewers is an essential and often overlooked part of the interview.

When asking questions, there are several things to keep in mind:

- **Prepare your questions in advance.** Do not count on asking questions off the cuff, or quality will often suffer. Under no circumstances should an interviewee say, "I have no questions for you." Always plan to ask questions.

- **Only ask open-ended questions to avoid them being answered yes or no.** Asking a yes-no question in an interview creates doubt if the interviewee is a deep analytical thinker. It also creates doubt if he is interested in the position.

- A good question makes the interviewer think for a second before answering. Also, make sure to listen carefully if his answer warrants a follow-up question. Do not tune out while the interviewer is talking—sometimes interviewers test the candidate by answering the question in an incomplete way and want to see if there is follow-up.

- **Make sure the questions are detailed and not something you could have found easily by yourself.**

  o For example, if you asked this:

What is the organizational structure of this position?

You risk the interviewers responding that the information exists on their company Web site and suggesting you review it.

DOUBT ALERT: If you ask a question that is easy to find on their Web site, you create the doubt how well you researched the job in advance. If you had reviewed the Web site you would have likely found the organizational chart.

o   A better question might be this:

I noticed on your Web site that your company is organized into three divisions. What do you consider to be the most important aspects of this divisional relationship with the other two areas?

This will demonstrate that you reviewed the Web site for preliminary research and shows that you are asking for more in-depth information.

- **Ask at least one question that comes from the content of the interview itself.** Although I earlier suggested having all questions written in advance, this is one circumstance where a question is formulated *during* the interview itself. Few candidates will actually do this during the interview, and it positively sets them apart from the competition for the job.

    o   Asking a question from the content of the interview itself requires the candidate to listen carefully during the interview and write a question that only could have been answered by being at the interview. As discussed in the Notes Page section, this question would be written in section C. (see page 50)

o   Example question:

You mentioned earlier that the department is looking at adding new software. Can you expand on how you plan to measure the success of this software?

- Another common question is "When will you be making your decision?" This question is usually answered by the interviewers themselves, but it is OK to ask if it's not covered. However, this should be the last question you ask.

Common mistakes when asking questions

- **Not listening carefully.** This happens when you ask a question that was already covered during the interview.

    DOUBT ALERT: You may be seen as a poor listener.

- **Asking too many questions.** Ideally, you want to ask a maximum of two to three questions. Asking too many questions risks annoying the interviewers and can create doubt about being respectful of their time.

- **Asking too long a question.** The questions should be straightforward and direct. This is not the time to try to impress the interviewer with a long and overly complicated question.

- **Name-dropping with your questions.** This can be a temptation if you have a high-level contact you want the interviewer to know about. In addition to being tacky and self-serving, asking a question like this can create doubt that you believe who you know is more important than what you know. Few managers want to hire a political gamer into their departments.

o   Example:

I mentioned to your chief financial officer I was applying for a job here, and he wished me luck. I know him through his son who was my roommate in college. Do you report to him?

In summary:

• Prepare two to three good questions in advance that you could not research easily. This will show that you have done some background work prior to the interview.

• Ask questions that require more than a yes-no answer. The more thought required by the interviewer, the better. But don't try to stump the interviewer with an overly complicated question either.

• Ask at least one question from the content of the interview itself. This is impressive and conveys you are a good and engaged listener.

• Don't name-drop at any time during the interview. It is rarely successful and often backfires.

• Listen carefully during the interview—don't ask a question that was already covered by the interviewers.

Job Search—How to Ask Questions in an Interview

Interview for a Customer Service Job—Questions to Ask in an Interview

Rachel should ask questions specific to the actual job duties. She can inquire about software used in the company and how it relates to the position. She should refer to previous knowledge of customer service to show she understands the working environment (learned through job shadowing).

Interview for an Analyst Job—Questions to Ask in an Interview

Thi should be asking questions surrounding the process of the job assignment. These questions include methodology to produce software or business documents, building on her research from job shadowing or other sources. Thi could also ask company-specific questions.

Interview for a Sales Job—Questions to Ask in an Interview

Unlike the customer service or analyst job, Steve should be prepared to discuss compensation with his position if it has not been covered already. Common questions include asking about commission structure, overall compensation package, and expense policy. Asking these questions can remove doubt that the job candidate is unfamiliar with the sales position and its often unique salary structure.

Common Closing Question: "What Else Do You Want to Share?"

A good closing prevents you from forgetting to share an important issue and helps summarize your skills.

While "Tell me about yourself" is an important first impression question, the closing question is a last chance to set the tone of the ending of the interview.

The closing question often sounds like "Is there anything else you'd like to tell us?" or "Do you have any closing comments?" Similar to the opening question, it is unfortunately often not prepared in advance, and it often shows.

At this stage of the interview, many candidates are typically tired and can appear short of energy. I have seen interviewees looking completely exhausted and seem "eager" to end the interview. However, it is important to show energy and enthusiasm at the closing to reiterate the reasons for hiring you and to remove any last remaining doubts. Make sure you save a little energy for the end of an interview!

A good closing reinforces the theme of why the candidate should be offered the position as well as targets removing any lingering doubt in his or her abilities.

Key parts of the closing include the following:
- Thanking the interviewers for their time and the opportunity to interview for the position. This shows sincerity and is considered professional.
- Reemphasize your interest in the job. Remarkably, many candidates appear to lack enthusiasm for the job opportunity at the end of the interview, which creates doubt about the passion for the role. *Make sure the interviewers know you want the position.*
- Focus on one or two primary experiences to highlight rather than a summary of all your experiences.
- It can be a great opportunity to discuss anything that wasn't asked during the interview but you want to make sure

is discussed. By reviewing your competency list (on the Notes Page discussed on page 50) you can see if any good experiences were omitted that you want covered.

- Keep it short.

Sample Closing:

Thank you again for the opportunity of an interview for (the position). I am very interested in the assignment and believe my background makes me well qualified to perform the duties that are required.

As I shared earlier, I have dedicated my life to the printing industry in various capacities and understand the unique challenges in this ever-changing business. I feel my twenty years of experience in manufacturing and more specifically my thirteen years as plant manager give me the experience needed for this important position. As I discussed, I have experience with all the latest direct-to-plate technologies as well as the amazing new hexachrome printing processes that are revolutionizing the business.

After this chance to discuss the position with you, I am more convinced than ever that this opportunity is a perfect fit for me and I welcome the challenge to serve your growing company.

One additional experience I did not have the chance to share in this interview is my eight years serving on the International Printing Board. This experience has given me great insight into the printing industry around the globe, as well as the enormous challenges facing our business as a whole. I would like to continue in this capacity if offered the position with your company, as it would help bring you the latest printing news.

I am looking forward to hearing from you, and thanks again for your time and consideration.

In summary, make sure your closing makes the case for you to get the job.

- Thank the interviewers for the opportunity for you to be interviewed. (Remarkably this often gets forgotten.)

- Restate your interest in the position. Show enthusiasm!

- Briefly highlight your top experiences that make you a strong candidate for the job.

- Review any additional information you neglected to cover during the interview.

- Emphasize that you are eager to hear from the interviewers.

Checklist

- Practice writing the "conclusion."

Thank the interviewers for their time: _____

_____

_____

_____

Restate your interest in the position: _____

_____

_____

_____

Highlight relevant (or other) experience: _____

_____

_____

_____

Emphasize you are eager to hear from the interviewers:

_____

_____

_____

Common Errors and Solutions in an Interview

There is no such thing as an error-free interview although the goal is obviously to minimize mistakes as much as possible. Mistakes occur during all phases of the interview process, not just during the interview itself. On most occasions, mistakes create doubt in the interviewer's eyes.

Listed below are common mistakes and potential solutions:

BEFORE THE INTERVIEW

- **Showing up late for the interview**

    o   Q: What if you are stuck in traffic and will likely be late for the interview? Should you:

1   call and explain you are running late but say you should only be a few minutes tardy?
2   not call and hope to get there close to the interview time? Most interviews don't start on time anyway.
3   call and explain you are running a little late and offer to reschedule the interview?

    o   A: In almost all occasions, *answer 3* is the correct one. By offering to reschedule you are respecting the interviewer's time and letting her decide if being late is OK with her schedule. If you will be more than thirty minutes late it is to your advantage to reschedule since your interview duration may be impacted. Answer 2 is never correct, and answer 1 risks that you will not arrive in only a few minutes and need to call back again with a new expected time of arrival.

- **Being impolite to the secretary or receptionist**

    o   Being polite should be obvious when applying for a job, but some job candidates think the charm needs to begin when they enter the interview room. As a result, interviewees sometimes act condescending to the secretary or scheduler prior to the interview. What the interviewee does not realize is that the real interview starts when he enters the building or is speaking on the phone to anyone in the company, not just with those in the interview room. Feedback for an interview candidate can come from the least expected sources.

- **Failing to research the job or company in advance**

   o   It is obvious to most job interviewers if a candidate did his homework. Advance research is *critical* to making the best impression and removing doubt. For more information on this topic see the chapter on Networking, page 29.

- **Not having a good meal before the interview**

   o   Eating a good meal before the interview is critical to keep your wits sharp and stomach from growling.

      ▪   Avoid eating too much. It can make you lethargic or sleepy during the interview.

      ▪   Avoid eating too little. You will burn calories during the intensity of an interview, so have enough fuel stored. For long interviews (over two hours), this is even more important and can prevent the dreaded growling stomach.

      ▪   Avoid eating salty food. It can dry out your mouth and make you thirsty. It may not be possible to get something to drink before the interview, and you may end up getting dry mouth.

      ▪   Avoid eating spicy or garlicky food. Bad breath is never good in an interview.

      ▪   Avoid drinking too much before an interview. It can be dangerous, especially with carbonated or caffeinated drinks. It can cause embarrassing burps or cause you to talk faster, if you are affected by caffeine. Drinking too much of any beverage can cause other obvious perils during a long interview.

- Do not chew gum during the interview. Remove any gum prior to entering the interview room.
- Limit any smoking prior to an interview. The smell can often can stay on your clothing and, depending on the interviewer, it can make a bad impression.
- *Never* drink alcohol before an interview. This can include even the night before the interview if it affects your performance the next day.

DURING THE INTERVIEW

- **Asking bad questions during the interview**

  o Asking bad questions during an interview is a common and avoidable mistake (see page 87, What Questions to Ask in an Interview). Examples of bad questions to the interviewers include the following:

    - **Asking about a proposed work schedule with an emphasis on time off**

      - This creates doubt if you are more interested in leisure time than the job duties.

    - **Asking how many candidates are vying for the job**

      - Although this sounds like a harmless question, it can create doubt that you are worried about your competition and can show a lack of confidence. Whether the company is interviewing two or ten, if you are the best candidate it should not matter about the competition.

- **Referring to any sports-related items**

  - If the interviewer's allegiance is to another sports team your fan support could inadvertently backfire.

- **Asking the interviewer about his or her job history at the company**

  - This popular question is often considered harmless and even flattering to let the interviewer talk about themselves. However, this question to the interviewer has three major drawbacks:
    - It takes valuable time away from the interview, focusing on someone else rather than talking about you.
    - If the interviewer has a dramatically different background from yourself, it could reinforce the doubt if you have the right qualifications and experience for this job based on the interviewee's background.
    - It may sound like you are trying to make the interviewer prove that she is "worthy" of interviewing you.

- **Taking a cell phone into the interview**

  o Q: What if you have to remain in contact with family due to a potential medical emergency during the interview? Should you:

    1. Take the cell phone into the interview and explain to the interviewers the reason you need to have it with you and the potential to be interrupted?
    2. Take the cell phone into the interview but put it on vibrate setting so it doesn't disturb the interview?
    3. Not take the cell phone with you or turn it off? Instead, leave the receptionist or secretary's phone number with your family, and let the interviewers know that you may need to be interrupted in the interview?

o   A: *Answer 3* is the correct one. This offers you the option to be contacted in an emergency but without the risk of a cell phone in the interview. Answer 1 is incorrect because it is possible others who have your cell number may attempt to call you during the interview. Answer 2 is incorrect because a vibrating cell phone can still be annoying.

- **Having poor nonverbal communication**

  o   There are many examples of nonverbal communications to avoid:

  - Fidgeting of any kind. This includes playing with pens, your hair, or any other item. It is distracting and annoying to the interviewer.
  - Excessive or nonexistent eye contact. Too much eye contact can look creepy; too little makes you appear disinterested or unsure in the interview.

- Poor posture. Sitting too comfortably shows disrespect. Sitting too rigidly makes you appear stiff and unfriendly.
- Looking at your watch during the interview. It conveys that you want to end the interview quickly (which may be true). Leave the watch in your pocket to reduce any temptation to look at it. Make sure to turn off any watch alarms.

- **Bad answers to questions**

  o A common error made during the interview occurs when the candidate does not have a good answer to a question.

  o Q: What should you do if you do not have a good answer to a behavior-based question that asks you to share an example from your past experiences?

   1. Make up an example that did not happen but demonstrates your competencies well and sound as convincing as possible?
   2. Admit to not having a real example but share what you *would* do if such a situation were to happen in the future?
   3. Admit to not having a real example that matches their question and ask for another question.

  o A: Answer 1 is wrong 100 percent of the time. Fabricating an answer is dangerous and often the candidate is caught creating enormous (and possibly fatal) doubt. Answer 2 will work if you ask permission to take that approach. You could say, "I don't have a specific example that answers that question, but I do have thoughts on how I would handle that situation if it ever arose. Is it OK to talk if I talk about that?" If the interviewer only wants *real* examples, the only viable choice is answer 3. This can be difficult to admit not having a good answer, but it is always better than fabricating an example.

- **Not dressing appropriately for the interview (wearing sweaters, underdressing, overdressing)**

  o   There are entire magazine articles dedicated to the subject of what to wear to a job interview. Although I am not a fashion critic, there are some common mistakes with apparel.

  ▪   Wearing a sweater to the interview. Even in the winter, you risk overheating during the interview. Wear cooler clothes as if you plan for the room to be warmer. Your interview nerves can make the room feel five degrees warmer.

  ▪   Overdressing for the interview. Conventional wisdom is to wear the best clothes you own to an interview. In reality, the goal of the interview is to remove doubt and not to win a fashion contest. Wear good clothes but appropriate for the job you are applying for, so the interviewers can visualize you in the role. If you overdress, they may have trouble seeing you in the role. If suits are standard clothes in the business you are being interviewed, you should dress in your best suit. If the dress code is casual, you can wear nice business casual without necessarily needing a tie or dress. Do research in advance to see what clothes are appropriate.

- Underdressing for the interview. Being too casual in the apparel is equally bad. It is always easier to remove a coat to fit in the relaxed atmosphere versus being awkward as the only person without a coat in the interview!
- Wearing uncomfortable clothes is a common mistake. Always try your clothes and any new shoes on before the interview! Remember to remove the tags from new clothes.

AFTER THE INTERVIEW

- **Not sending a thank-you note or sending one with misspellings. (See "Thank-You Notes," page 112.)**

  o You should always send thank-you notes after an interview. However, there are some common mistakes with the note:

  - Misspelling the names of the interviewers. Double-check spelling of names and titles (use Notes Page to capture interviewers' names).
  - E-mailing a note. Handwriting a note is generally better than an e-mailed thank-you note. A handwritten note is more personal and stands out from the regular e-mail traffic of the interviewer.
  - Sending the thank-you card too late. It should be sent within twenty-four hours after the interview. If you are applying in a new company, mail the

note. If you are applying for a new position within a company where you are already employed, send the thank-you note through interoffice mail.

- Having sloppy handwriting. Take your time writing the thank-you note. The interviewer should not struggle to read your scribbles.

- Typing a thank-you note. Unless you are sending an e-mail (which is not the preferred method), always handwrite the note and sign it. Typing a thank-you note card looks sterile and impersonal.

- Sending the same thank-you note wording to all interviewers. Personalize each thank-you note for each interviewer. Sometimes they share the cards, and writing the same comments in different notes is tacky.

Game Plan for the Interview

A successful interview needs to be both well planned and well executed. The game plan for the interview itself includes the following:

- Using a theme-based answer approach to the opening "Tell me about yourself" question. This is more effective than the traditional "oral resume" many people use for this question (page 72).

- Answering behavior-based questions using the hourglass answer style. It contains the important information in the beginning, the details in the middle, and a strong conclusion restating the results. This is much better than the chronological approach to answering questions, which often has the important results only at the end of the question (page 76).

- Watching your body language and the body language of the interviewers. If you believe by what you are observing that you are creating doubt, try to identify and address the doubt (page 83).

- Having good questions prepared in advance of the interview. These questions should be thought provoking and should demonstrate the extensive research you have conducted prior to the interview (page 87).

- Ensuring your closing is well planned and restates why you should be hired for the job (page 92).

The next section provides important (and often overlooked) steps after the interview is over.

After the Interview

After the Interview

Once the interview is completed, it is important to learn from your experience and also send the thank-you notes. Listed below are the steps in this section of the interview planning process:

- Postevaluation Debrief (What Worked, What Didn't)

- The All-Important Thank-You Note

- What to Do If You Didn't Get the Job

Postevaluation Debrief (What Worked, What Didn't)

The last thing most interview candidates want to do is relive a recently concluded interview. Having survived the interview, the first reaction is to avoid thinking about it and hope for the best. However, there are key steps that need to be accomplished right after the interview to capture what did and did not work well, so that you can improve in the next interview. I call this the *postevaluation debrief*.

Right after the interview, find a quiet area away from the interviewers. Review and document how you feel the interview went. You should do the postreview as soon as possible after the interview when your memory is the freshest.

Using your Notes Page as a reference, review what questions you answered well and ones that did not go as well. You will need to rely somewhat on the body language of the interviewers and their follow-up questions to ascertain their thoughts.

o   If you seemed to answer a question well, make note of your answer. This is one you should use in a future interview if applicable.

o   If an answer seemed to go poorly, target that answer for replacement. Refer to your Kudos File (page 37) for another answer that might work better.

o   If you did not know the answer to a question that was asked, make sure you note it for follow-up to get the answer. I have known candidates who could not answer a difficult question asked in an interview and did not follow-up later to find the answer. To their surprise, they were asked the very same question in another interview.

o   A sample postevaluation debrief is shown on the next page. It is a simple way to learn how to improve for your next interview.

POSTEVALUATION DEBRIEF SAMPLE

Interview date: _____ / _____ / _____

Position: _____

Company/Department: _____

_____

Questions that went well:

_____

_____

_____

Questions that went poorly:

_____

_____

_____

Next steps:

_____

_____

_____

The All-Important Thank-You Note

One of the least expensive steps in the interview process is the thank-you note. Remarkably, many candidates do not send thank-you notes to the interviewers. Candidates are often afraid if they send a thank-you note, they will "look like they are trying to influence the interviewers," and it could create a negative perception.

Thank-you notes are an important way to show appreciation to the interviewers and get your name across their desks again. These should be sent to mock interviewers, job shadowers, mentors, and anyone else who has assisted you in the job quest.

Features of a good thank-you note:

- The note should be short and avoid restating qualifications for the position. Although it can be sent by e-mail, a handwritten note is best and will avoid getting lost in the interviewer's clogged e-mail.

- The note should reemphasize your interest in the job.

- It should be sent within twenty-four hours of the interview so as to be timely.

- It should be mailed if you are applying to a new company. If you are interviewed within your current company, it can be sent through interoffice mail.

- The thank-you notes should be legible. Take your time to write neatly. This includes addressing the envelope.

- Thank-you notes should be sent to all interviewers. However, do not write the same note to multiple interviewers. They sometimes compare the notes.

- Keep track of who you sent them to. Sometimes you inadvertently send repeat thank-you notes to the same person.

- Make sure all interviewers' names are spelled correctly!

A sample thank-you note is in appendix D (page 126).

What to Do If You Didn't Get the Job

There are many reasons why someone is not selected for a position after an interview, and they are not always what the interviewers "officially" tell the candidate in the rejection letter. Often, it is up to the interviewee to determine whether it was his or her background qualifications (someone was better qualified), interview performance, or a combination of the two that primarily caused the candidate to not be selected for a position.

As disappointing as it may be to receive a rejection letter, there are things you can do to learn from the experience and be a better interview candidate the next time.

There are some myths about failing to get the job in the interview:

- **Myth #1: You can't really prepare for an interview. It's all based on luck, and nothing you do in advance can improve your chances of getting the job.**

  o Nothing could be farther from the truth. Failure to receive a job offer doesn't necessarily mean you prepared poorly; it likely means that someone else prepared better than you did or had stronger job qualifications. The goal is to *learn* from your mistakes and not repeat them.

  o One technique is to use the postevaluation debrief (discussed on page 110) to outline what worked well and what didn't work in the interview. This is valuable even if you receive a job offer, so you can learn what to do better for any future interviews.

- **Myth #2: You can't learn from a bad interview. It's better to forget about it.**

  o Although it is tempting to try and forget a bad interview experience, it is a golden opportunity to learn from your mistakes and be better prepared the next time.

- Based on feedback from the interview, adapt your examples and approach to the interview. Try to determine what doubt remained during the interview so you can form a plan to address it before the next interview.

For example, if the interviewers asked repeated clarifying questions about your work experience, there may be a doubt that you articulated your work history completely. Review your answers and see how you can be more specific regarding previous job experience that addresses any doubts in this area.

- **Myth #3: If the interviewers rejected me once, they will never want to hire me.**

  o This emotional response is quite natural given the rejection of a job interview. However, I have seen many examples where a rejection did not eliminate the chance to get another position in the same company.

    - One unique approach that has worked in the past is to send a note to the interviewers after you receive the rejection letter thanking them again for the interview and asking for any constructive feedback to learn from the interview. Although this may seem awkward, I know someone who did this and impressed the interviewers so much, they routed her resume to another department who offered her an open position. Note: This only works if you feel the interview went very well. If you believe the interview did not go well, this approach may antagonize the interviewers.

There are very few people who have not received a rejection letter at some point in their careers. Besides being damaging to the ego, they often leave the interview candidates frustrated and angry. The best approach is to learn from your mistakes in removing doubt and realize there is always the next interview to be better prepared for.

Conclusion

The goal of this book was to share a new way to approach the job interview from the perspective of targeting and removing doubt. Most interviewers will tell you that they hire the person they are most confident will perform the job well—the one they have the fewest doubts about.

As the interview candidate, it is your mission to identify any doubts in advance, address those doubts, and not create new doubts during the interview itself.

This approach has several advantages:

- It helps you focus on removing any doubts with the interviewer.
- It gets to the root of the job interview by seeing if you are the best candidate. If there are major doubts you cannot remove while preparing for the interview, it may be a sign that this is the wrong job for you.
- It offers tools and a plan to prepare for the job interview by aligning your examples to competencies. These tools (like the Kudos File) have uses outside the interview to help with job performance reviews.
- It can be an effective way to organize your thoughts before the interview and have a memory assistant during the interview.
- It can dramatically improve the communication of answers through use of the hourglass answer technique.
- It offers the chance to learn from the process and improve for any future interviews.

I hope the tools in this book can assist you in your job search and help you remove doubt you can get the job you want.

APPENDIX A

Doubts Created and How to Combat Them

BACKGROUND RESUME INFO	PERCEPTION TO INTERVIEWERS/ POTENTIAL DOUBT	WAYS TO MITIGATE THE DOUBT
Poor grades in college or formal education.	Could give perception that candidate is unfocused or not able to finish assigned tasks. Doubts around quality of work performed and pride in work completed.	Emphasize learning outside of formal education and a genuine love of learning. Give examples of completion of tasks with quality.
Very high grades in college or formal education.	Depending on other personality traits, could give the perception of being a perfectionist or being arrogant. Candidate could need a constant diet of accolades to be motivated. Possible impression of being a loner and more interested in personal achievement.	Limit reference to grades. They are on the resume, and the interviewers are aware of them. Instead, discuss accomplishments within the team and business results. Avoid appearing to need or want kudos for accomplishing tasks.
Lack of formal education/training	Can give perception of poor learning habits or difficulty in training. Can also appear not dedicated to education or continual improvement of skills.	Do not apologize for lack of formal education or give reasons/excuses. Emphasize non-formal education and its role in personal development. Make sure answers note a love of learning and self-improvement. Depending on career, can discuss your desire for future education.

BACKGROUND RESUME INFO	PERCEPTION TO INTERVIEWERS/ POTENTIAL DOUBT	WAYS TO MITIGATE THE DOUBT
Lack of experience in job area.	Gives perception of lack of knowledge of business area. Concerns about training needed and ability to learn.	Emphasize similar types of experiences and ability to learn quickly. Do not apologize for lack of experience, but change the focus to your ability to learn and cite examples where you were successful beginning a job with little experience.
Appearance of job-hopping/ short tenure at jobs.	Perception of not being able to hold a job. Doubts about longevity and dedication to a career. Doubts about holding attention span and tendency to get bored with a job after a short time.	Do not hide the fact you have had many assignments. Give examples around your variety of experiences and how they rounded your background. Emphasize your desire to settle down and make a career at this company.
Longevity and one job or assignment.	Can give the appearance of fear to take risks or learn something new. Also could show a conservative nature and uneasiness with change.	Give examples of the variety of assignments within the same company or job title. Discuss how you enjoy learning new things and can handle change.

Doubts created during the interview can be due to the interviewee's personality or speaking style. It is critical in this evaluation for the interviewee to accurately determine how his or her words are being perceived (what the interviewers are hearing). A mock interview can be an excellent way to identify these traits.

PERSONALITY TRAIT	PERCEPTION TO INTERVIEWERS/ POTENTIAL DOUBT	WAYS TO MITIGATE THE DOUBT
Assertive personality. Appears overconfident.	Interviewee will be hard to manage/not take criticism well. Will not like being led on a team and will not follow or take direction easily.	Make sure answers talk about flexible/team-oriented side. Show a vulnerable side so they know interviewer sees you take criticism and act on it.
Too business focused. All answers resemble a court interrogation.	Not team player. May have poor interpersonal skills and be hard to manage.	Talk about how you enjoy working on a team. Give examples of successes you had as part of a team.
Too giddy/nervous during interview. Laughs too much or has voice inflection that is too high.	Not serious about the job. Doubt about your professionalism and dedication.	Emphasize your business approach with examples. Show with examples that you are serious and dedicated about the job.
Talks too much. Answers are cumbersome and overdetailed.	Perceived to dominate interactions with others. Doubt of being hard to manage and ability to work well with a team. Also more interested in talking and may be a poor listener.	Listen carefully during the interview and do not interrupt the interviewer during questions. Give an example of how you listened to an alternative opinion and acted on it.
Talks too little during interview. Answers are short and incomplete.	Perception that interviewee may not have much to contribute. May lead to questioning intellect if answers appear simple or not well thought-out. Doubts about how well prepared the candidate was for the interview.	Ensure answers have substance, even if brief. In asking questions of the interviewer, ask detailed, thought-provoking question that required you to have completed extensive research. Use hourglass method (see page 76).

PERSONALITY TRAIT	PERCEPTION TO INTERVIEWERS/ POTENTIAL DOUBT	WAYS TO MITIGATE THE DOUBT
Vague answers.	Interviewee appears unfocused, not prepared for the interview. Doubts about ability to plan/lead an initiative.	Plan out answers in advance. Give examples of when you planned a project or how your organization led to the project's success.
Loud voice.	May appear overbearing and have potential team conflicts. Doubts around team dynamics and potential inability to manage the person.	Practice being softer-spoken. In the interview discuss how you successfully worked "under" someone else.
Quiet voice.	Could appear timid/not standing up for issues. Doubts around demonstrating leadership in challenging situations.	Practice before the interview being more clear, forceful, and deliberate in answers. In interview discuss examples when you took the lead on a project.
Nervous/voice shakes during interview.	Perception interviewee won't work well under pressure and may not seek out difficult assignments.	When sharing examples, talk about successfully handling stressful situations. Emphasize desire for, and lack of fear with, challenging assignments to compensate for your nerves.
Bad posture/too casual posture during interview.	Gives perception the interviewee is not serious about the job. Depending on other personality traits could appear too confident (i.e. certain to get the job).	Practice good posture and not looking too informal during the interview. When answering questions, don't be glib or informal.
"Military-style" or rigid posture.	May appear inflexible, hard-nosed and procedure-focused. Difficult to manage or appear to be not team-oriented.	Show your softer side. Give examples of when showed a creative or flexible side at work. Make sure your voice is not loud or dominating as it may reinforce the doubt about your flexibility.

PERSONALITY TRAIT	PERCEPTION TO INTERVIEWERS/ POTENTIAL DOUBT	WAYS TO MITIGATE THE DOUBT
Tendency to ramble and/or be a person that will chew up the managers' time getting to the point.	Could indicate lack of focus. The interviewee may ignore important details on work assignments.	Practice giving short, to the point stories prior to the interview. Give examples about showing focus and accomplishing tasks.
Making too much eye contact.	Gives perception of challenging the interviewer. Potentially hard to manage or unfriendly. Can also appear to be unwilling to take criticism or suggestions.	When giving answers, give examples of how you followed the advice of others. Give the perception that you are open-minded and willing to receive feedback. Soften your tone and choice of words.
Making too little eye contact.	May appear timid and won't challenge bad ideas. Could also appear not ready for this new job/assignment.	Give examples of how you professionally challenged authority. Give answers with confident wording.
Physically shakes during the interview due to nerves (not caused by medical condition).	Can make the candidate not look strong or able to handle pressure.	Hold hands in your lap or on table to control observable shaking.
Asking questions about salary or talking about monetary rewards from previous job. (Can be acceptable interviewing for a sales position.)	Gives perception that motivation is solely financial. Doubts could be created that only monetary reinforcement will work. Concern candidate will quickly leave current job seeking more money elsewhere.	Counter any perceptions by discussing nonmonetary aspects of the job.

APPENDIX B

Interview Notes Page Template

A—List the names of the interviewers here in the order they are sitting across from you. *(Write **during** the interview.)*

B—List the questions you are ASKING the interviewers. (Have three to four questions ready.) *(Write **before** interview and leave space for their response.)*	D—List competencies and examples here. Use a few words to trigger your memory. *(Write **before** interview.)*
C—Write a question that comes from the *interview* itself. *(Write **during** interview.)*	E—List any other information you would like to share. *(Write **before** interview.)*

APPENDIX C

Postevaluation Debrief Sample

Interview date: _____ / _____ / _____

Position: _____

Company/Department: _____

_____

Questions that went well:

_____

_____

_____

Questions that went poorly:

_____

_____

_____

Next steps:

_____

_____

_____

APPENDIX D

Sample Thank-you Note

Dear Mr. Jones:

Thank you for the opportunity to be interviewed as a billing analyst for _____ Company. I enjoyed meeting you and speaking with you about the position.

I am very excited about the position and look forward to hearing from you soon.

Sincerely,

INDEX